# Regiments at Waterloo

# Regiments at Waterloo

## Vol 2  British Army Uniforms

### René North

**ALMARK**

*Almark Publishing Co. Ltd., London*

# THE ANGLO-ALLIED ARMY

*'It all depends upon that article'*
*Wellington, pointing to a British soldier*

Of about 97,000 men in the Allied armies at Waterloo, it may seem a little surprising that less than a third of that number were indigenous British troops, the rest being composed of Hanoverians, Dutch-Belgians, Brunswickers and Nassauers – to say nothing of the not inconsiderable contingent of The King's German Legion.

The Prussians, under Field-Marshal Blücher, have not been considered here, because the intention is to limit the subject to Wellington's command, which after all bore the brunt of the fighting. True, but for the timely arrival of the Prussians towards evening, the result might well have been different; but the fact remains that they were a separate entity and cannot be reckoned as an integral part of the Allied army. Nor should it be forgotten that when Blücher's 116,000 troops arrived, Napoleon found himself outnumbered by almost 2 to 1.

In the British army, new dress regulations had appeared in 1811, whose main effect was to introduce a totally new uniform for the Light Dragoons and an infantry shako with a high false front supposedly of 'belgic' derivation, which became known later as the 'Waterloo shako'. It had a short life, incidentally, because in 1816 it was replaced by one of bell-topped shape.

Non-commissioned officers' badges of rank, in the familiar chevron form, were worn on the right sleeve only (except in the Light Infantry), above the elbow. They were in white lace for sergeants and in regimental lace for corporals. The lance-corporal appeared at about this time, but his particular badge, if any, is not clear. (The name, derived from the French *l'ansepessade*, originated in turn from the Spanish *lanza pesada*. This denoted a cavalryman who had lost his mount in battle and therefore joined a foot unit, still carrying his lance. Being a horseman, he was superior to a mere foot-soldier, but inferior to a non-commissioned officer: hence the appointment, but not the rank, of lance-corporal.)

The British musket was the famous 'Brown Bess', whose chief difference from the French weapon was the absence of the two metal collars securing the barrel to the wooden stock.

The cavalry swords were of two patterns: straight for the heavy regiments and curved for the light.

Horse-furniture in the heavy cavalry consisted mostly of a sheepskin or blanket, with a scarlet cloak rolled and strapped over the pommel, and a scarlet valise at the back. In the light branch, a blue shabraque was used, with a round valise of the same colour, both items having a border in either yellow or white according to the buttons. (This can be taken as fairly general for all armies, since the colour of lace, loops, hat-ornaments, etc., are usually based on the same principle.)

British field officers wore two epaulettes and subalterns one only, on the right shoulder, while all had crimson sashes; and here again the metal of the epaulettes agreed with the buttons and loops.

# Household Cavalry



The British Household troops, counterparts of the French Imperial Guard, consisted of no more than three regiments of cavalry and a like number of infantry, in marked contrast with the vast numbers of their opposite body.

The cavalry regiments were the 1st and 2nd Life Guards and the Royal Horse Guards. The first of these were descended from a corps of cavalier gentlemen raised by Charles II in 1660, and still take precedence over every other regiment in the army, unless the Royal Horse Artillery is present with its guns.

The 2nd Life Guards, also raised in 1660, were first styled 'The Duke of Albermarle's Troop of Guards'. In 1670 they became known as 'The Queen's Troop of Life Guards', but it was not until 1788 that the title of 2nd Life Guards was granted.

The Royal Horse Guards are more ancient still, since the regiment claims its origin from the Civil War, when it was a regiment of horse in the Parliamentarian forces. It was consequently to have been disbanded at the Restoration of 1660, but the King gave orders for its immediate re-establishment, and, contrary to the 2nd Life Guards, it has remained in existence ever since.

At Waterloo, the Life Guards wore red jackets with a dark blue collar-patch and turnbacks, and blue-grey overalls with a scarlet band. The lace and girdle were yellow, the latter bearing two crimson stripes, while the helmet had brass fittings, a black-over-crimson crest and a white plume. The 1st Life Guards wore yellow shoulder-straps and the 2nd blue, but for the rest the uniforms were identical.

The Royal Horse Guards were not officially recognized as Household Cavalry until 1820, but were nevertheless brigaded with the Life Guards. As such they assisted, with the rest of the Brigade, in repulsing the French counter-attack which developed after the charge of the Union Brigade. Their uniform, of the same pattern of the Life Guards, was dark blue with scarlet facings.

*(1) Corporal of Horse. 1st Life Guards. All helmet-fittings, including the peak, were brass; and the frontal plate carried the interlaced Royal Cypher surmounted by a crown. The collar was red, with dark blue patches, each bearing two yellow loops. Cuffs and shoulder-straps were dark blue, the former edged in yellow; the rank-stripes were gold.*

*(2) Trooper. Royal Horse Guards. The uniform is identical with the Life Guards' except that the jacket colours are reversed. The heavy cavalry sword was carried in a steel scabbard and a white sword-knot was attached to the hilt. It was a formidable weapon, intended for thrusting, with a wide blade.*

(3) Trooper. The Life Guards. Note the short-slung sabretache. The star was brass.

(4) Officer. The Life Guards. Shabraques were dark blue in the Life Guards, and scarlet in the Royal Horse Guards.

# Dragoon Guards





The title of Dragoon Guards originated in the early 18th century, when for reasons of economy several regiments of horse were converted to dragoons. They were thus to receive less pay than hitherto, but as a rather meagre compensation were allowed the title of Guards, although never forming an integral part of the Household troops.

The 1st The King's Dragoon Guards, senior Horse Regiment of the Line (Fig 1), was brigaded with the Household Cavalry and took part with the latter in the action in which they were attacked by Travers' 7th and 12th Cuirassiers in the Ohain road, west of the cross-roads. The attack was repulsed, but the British, in their elation, galloped too far in pursuit and were thus compelled to retreat hurriedly in the face of a vigorous counter-attack by fresh regiments of Cuirassiers. Of the 2,000 men who charged originally, a bare 1,200 or 1,300 regained their original position behind La Haye Sainte.

This famous regiment, raised in 1685, was dressed in the uniform laid down for heavy cavalry, when a rather unserviceable hat was replaced by a black leather helmet somewhat resembling the French in design, with its brass comb and horsehair streamer. The frontal plate, also of brass, bore the interlaced Royal Cypher, and the regimental title appeared in a small oval underneath.

The jacket was ornamented with two rows of yellow lace running down the front from the top edge of the collar to the bottom of the jacket, which was fastened by hooks and eyes, thereby excluding the presence of any buttons. The facings, as befitted a Royal regiment, were dark blue.

*(5) King's Dragoon Guards – Officer. Helmet, black leather with brass plates, crest and chin-chains, black horsehair mane. Jacket, scarlet with dark blue collar, cuffs and turnbacks, the front of the jacket and collar were edged with gold lace, the same lace on the top edge of the cuffs and on the turnback edges, this lace had a central stripe in the facing colour, gold cord on shoulders. White pouch belt, black pouch, the sword belt was worn over the gold and crimson waist sash overalls dark grey with a wide red stripe.*

*(6) King's Dragoon Guards – Trooper. The uniform details were similar to those given for the officer except that the lace was yellow and shoulder straps were worn on the jacket, these being dark blue with yellow cord edges, while the officers overalls only had leather cuffs round the bottom those for other ranks were reinforced inside the leg, the sabretache was of plain black leather.*

"

(7) Officer. The Royal Scots Greys. The cap-fittings are gold and the plume white. Jacket is scarlet with dark blue cuffs, collar and turnbacks, and gold lace. The sash is crimson, and the gloves and breeches white.

(8) Sergeant. The Royal Scots Greys. This is the service dress of the regiment, comprising blue-grey overalls with a dark blue band. Remainder as for officers, except yellow attributes where the officers' are gold. Note the gold sergeant's stripes on the right sleeve. At this period the regiment was also known as the North British Dragoons, and the initials NBD are carried on the saddle valise.

# Dragoons





If the King's Dragoon Guards were the only unit of that branch at Waterloo, the Dragoons were represented by three regiments: the 1st Royal Dragoons (Fig 2), the 2nd (Royal Scots Greys) and the 6th Inniskilling Dragoons – English, Scots and Irishmen forming the Union Brigade.

The 1st Dragoons was raised in 1661 for service in Tangier and originally wore cuirasses which were subsequently discarded. At Waterloo it was in the brigade which charged the French and galloped right into two divisional artillery batteries, and even reached Napoleon's Great Battery of 80 guns on its left. It was The Royals who attacked Bourgeois' 28th and 105th Regiments of the 1st Infantry Division.

The Royal Scots Greys were the only regular regiment of Scottish cavalry, and the only British cavalry regiment to wear the bearskin cap, granted in recognition of its capture of the Colours of the French *Régiment du Roi* at Ramillies in 1706.

Indeed, the feat was repeated at Waterloo in the memorable charge of the Union Brigade in which Sergeant Ewart took the Eagle of the 45th Line Regiment under Colonel Chapuzet, when the Greys, with Highlanders clinging to their stirrup-leathers, broke into Marcognet's 3rd Infantry Division with the exalted cry of 'Scotland for ever!'

The soldiers on the grey horses rightly earned the respect of their adversaries; and Napoleon's exclamation of *'Ces terribles chevaux gris'* was a fitting tribute to their bravery.

The third regiment of the Union Brigade, raised in 1689, became known as the '6th or Inniskilling Regiment of Dragoons' in the following year (Fig 3). At Waterloo, in the famous charge, its immediate objective was Donzelot's 2nd Infantry Division; but like its sister regiments, it penetrated too far into the enemy lines and came under a sharp counter-attack by the 3rd and 4th Chevaulégers-Lanciers. Fortunately, the 12th and 16th Light Dragoons were at hand and came to the rescue, thus enabling the survivors to regain their own lines in time.

This unit, not being a Royal regiment entitled to blue facings, wore yellow instead.

*(9) Dragoon Marching Order – Royal Scots Greys. Head-dress covered with black oilskin foul weather cover. Coat red with dark blue collar, cuffs, turnbacks and shoulder straps all edged with dragoon pattern yellow lace and cord. Girdle yellow with two blue stripes, over this was worn the white sword belt. Overalls grey lined inside with fawn coloured leather, a blue stripe on the legs with yellow metal buttons.*

*(10) Dragoon – Marching Order. The dress details are the same as for the Royal Scots Greys except for head-dress and regimental differences, for the 1st Dragoons the facing colour was the same dark blue with yellow lace, for the 6th Dragoons yellow facings with white lace. This figure shows the manner in which the equipment was carried, pouch and carbine belts over the left shoulder, haversack and wooden water bottle over the right.*

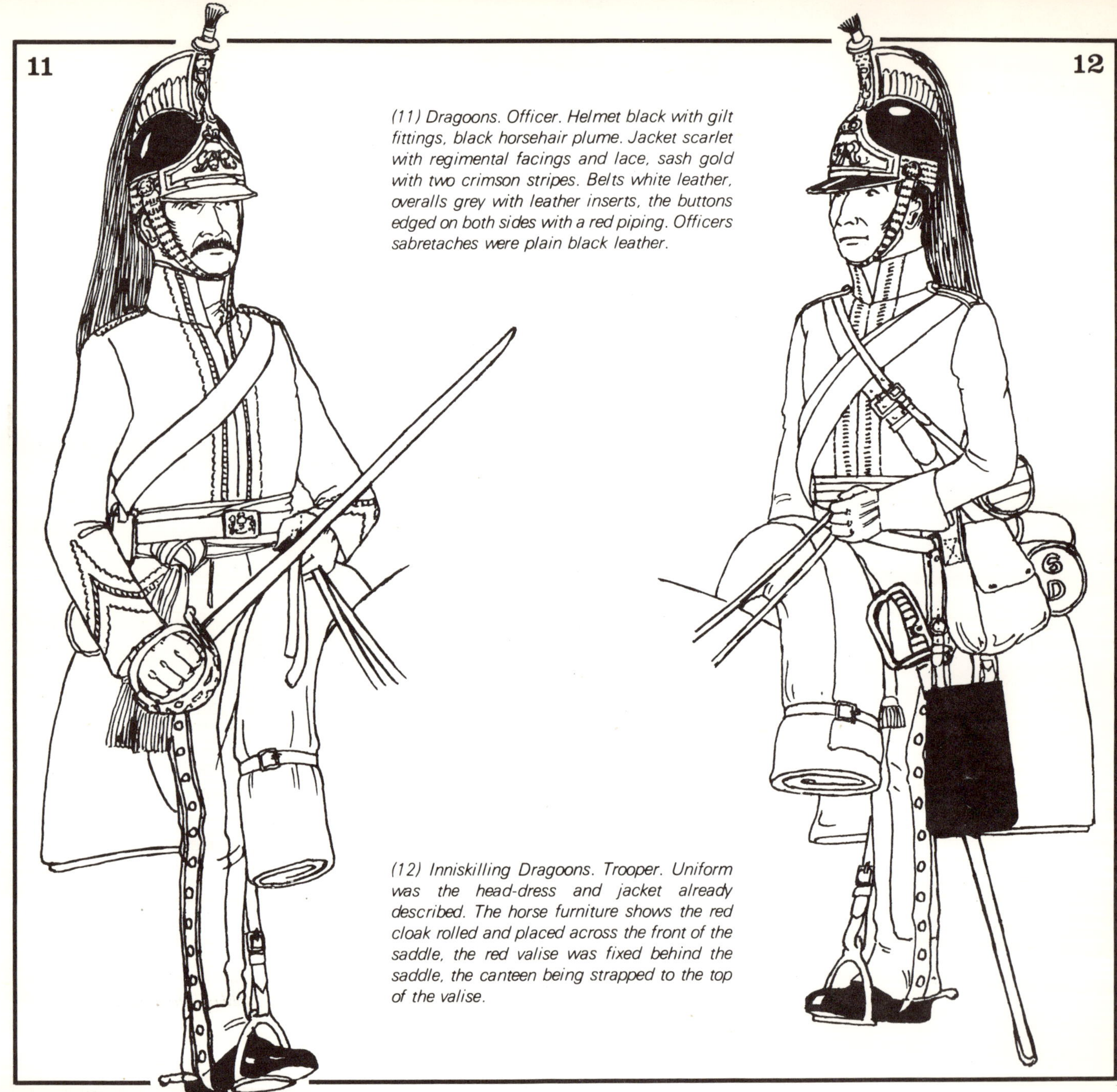





(11) Dragoons. Officer. Helmet black with gilt fittings, black horsehair plume. Jacket scarlet with regimental facings and lace, sash gold with two crimson stripes. Belts white leather, overalls grey with leather inserts, the buttons edged on both sides with a red piping. Officers sabretaches were plain black leather.

(12) Inniskilling Dragoons. Trooper. Uniform was the head-dress and jacket already described. The horse furniture shows the red cloak rolled and placed across the front of the saddle, the red valise was fixed behind the saddle, the canteen being strapped to the top of the valise.

# Light Dragoons




Light Dragoons were formed in the British Army when, about the middle of the 18th century, the need for light cavalry made itself felt and several existing regiments were converted to that arm.

In 1812 the uniform underwent a radical change. The former crested helmet was replaced by a bell-topped shako of French inspiration, and the blue laced jacket gave place to one of plainer design, with collar, lapels, cuffs and turn-backs in the facing colour, so that the five regiments present at Waterloo appeared as follows:

| Regiment | Facings and Girdle | Epaulettes | Buttons |
|---|---|---|---|
| 11th | buff | white | silver |
| 12th | yellow | white | silver |
| 13th | buff | yellow | brass |
| 16th | scarlet | white | silver |
| 23rd | crimson | white | silver |

The upper edge of the shako and the cap-lines were in the same colour as the epaulettes, and the girdle usually had two blue stripes lengthwise. White breeches and black hessian boots were worn on dress occasions, but in the field these were covered with blue-grey overalls normally bearing a double stripe in the facing colour. Shabraques were dark blue and, in most cases, carried ornaments in the facing colour.

For officers the dress was similar, except that their girdles were gold with two crimson stripes, and their cap-lines gold and crimson mixed. Epaulettes and suchlike attributes were gold or silver as the men's were yellow or white. The plume was white-over-red for all ranks, but whereas the officers carried sabretaches with gold or silver embroidery, the other ranks' pattern was plain black leather.

The 12th Light Dragoons was one of the regiments which came to the rescue of the Union Brigade, after their famous charge, by falling on the right flank of General Durutte's 4th Infantry Division (8th, 29th, 58th and 95th Line Regiments).

The regiment, raised in 1715, was one of those converted to Light Dragoons and served in India for an uninterrupted spell of 76 years.

It also took part in the Peninsular War, and it is from that period that the custom arose for the band to play hymns every evening at tattoo, allegedly as a punishment for breaking into a nunnery. Another, more probable version, however, is simply that Pope Pius VI presented the music to the regiment with the request that it should be played by the band.

The 13th was stationed west of the Brussels road, alongside the 15th Hussars and the 2nd

*(13) In full dress, officers wore white breeches and Hessian boots, but on active service these were replaced by blue-grey overalls, like the other ranks', with stripes in the facing colour (in this case, buff). (14) Private. 12th Light Dragoons. This soldier is in dress uniform. The plumes are always white-over-red for all regiments.*

Light Dragoons of the King's German Legion. However, it was withdrawn just before the heavy attack on Hougoumont by Milhaud's IVth Cavalry Corps and the Lefebvre-Desnoettes Light Cavalry of the Guard, consisting of eight Cuirassier regiments, with the Lancers, Chasseurs, Grenadiers and Dragoons of the Guard. It thus had the opportunity to harass the Cuirassiers swirling around the British squares, but was compelled to fall back when attacked by the main body.

The 16th, posted on the left of the line, was brigaded with the 12th and therefore assisted in the relief of the Union Brigade after their rather unfortunate charge. In that action the 16th defeated a regiment of French lancers, rode straight through a battery of artillery and put as many as 40 guns out of action.

Later in the day, the two brigades of light cavalry being still intact and in perfect order, the 16th, with the 12th on its right, took part in the large-scale attack when six regiments rode down a square of the Imperial Guard, as well as a large number of Cuirassiers and artillery, taking 3,000 prisoners. It was in this action that some German dragoons mistook the 16th for French troops (the blue jackets may easily have looked green in the poor light) and the regiment narrowly escaped being attacked in the rear, thus giving substance to Wellington's objection to the new uniform as being, as he put it, 'too frenchified'.

In fact, the new dress was not issued to the 16th until 1814 and many officers wore the old laced jacket at Waterloo. Captain Luard, however, states in his memoirs that he wore regulation uniform during the battle, but that his lapels were white, which seems odd. On the other hand, a contemporary print shows Cornet Polehill of the 16th in the old laced jacket, but wearing regulation dress for the remainder.

The 23rd Light Dragoons which was present at Waterloo was one of two regiments bearing the same number almost at the same time: an extraordinary and confusing piece of duplication. The present regiment was disbanded in 1817, but it is interesting to recall that it was one of the four selected for conversion to Lancers after the French troops of that arm had wrought such havoc in the Union Brigade.

**15**

*(15) Officer. 13th Light Dragoons. Taken from a print by Langendy, this figure wears somewhat unconventional shako-ornaments; and the overall-stripe should be double, for light cavalry. Note also the gold 'waterfall' at the centre of the back, below the girdle.*

# Hussars



The hussar branch of British light cavalry was not recognized officially until 1805, although the Prince Regent had already provided his own regiment, the 10th Light Dragoons, with many accoutrements of hussar pattern (Fig 5). Other regiments followed suit until authority finally had to concede the change, and eventually the 7th, 10th, 15th and 18th Light Dragoons were permitted rather grudgingly to call themselves Hussars and dress as such.

The Colonel of the 7th was the Marquess of Anglesey: the Lord Uxbridge of Waterloo fame. The 7th (Fig 4) had been very heavily engaged at Quatre Bras on June 16, and lost no fewer than 46 men on that day.

In the early stages of the battle of Waterloo the 10th Hussars were stationed on the left of the Allied line, on the right of the 11th, 12th and 16th Light Dragoons, when at about 12.30 a body of French troops advanced towards them. The 10th, however, was next moved to the centre, in support of the Brunswick Infantry, and towards the end of the battle, in company with the 18th and 1st Hussars of the King's German Legion, took part in Sir Hussey Vivian's final attacks on the enemy. These were probably the determining factor in the victory, for Sir Hussey, in a letter to a relative, says that the Commanding Officer of the 3rd Chasseurs of the Guard expressed the opinion that 'two regiments of British Hussars decided the affair'.

The 15th Hussars were descended from a regiment which acquired fame at the battle of Emsdorf, on June 16, 1760, when it defeated five battalions of French infantry and captured their Colours as well as nine guns. In recognition of that achievement the regiment was granted a lengthy battle honour stating the facts at length: a cumbersome feature later replaced by the device of crossed flags inverted, worn on the shabraque.

Another peculiarity of the regiment was the scarlet shako which was worn at Waterloo in lieu of the regulation busby (Fig 6). At the start of the battle, the regiment (brigaded with the 13th Light Dragoons) was stationed in first line at an angle in rear of Hougoumont Farm; but in the afternoon, after having withdrawn from that position, the 15th, together with the 13th, charged ten squadrons of French lancers. However, as it moved to the right it encountered a large body of Cuirassiers carrying all before them between Hougoumont and La Haye Sainte. The 15th and 13th immediately attacked, driving back the French cavalry and later took part in several other charges in the evening.

So far as the 18th Hussars are concerned (Fig 7), much private correspondence remains to inform us of their contribution to the fighting, from which one gathers that the regiment, with the 10th Hussars and the 1st Hussars of the King's German Legion, were in Sir Hussey Vivian's Brigade in position on the right of the lane leading to Verd Cocou, where they were used in support of the Nassauers and Brunswickers in the centre of the line. Later, the whole brigade was ordered forward towards La Belle Alliance, the 18th following the 10th, and the Germans in the rear. The 10th charged, and towards the evening the whole brigade encountered the French Imperial Guard: squares of infantry with Chasseurs à Cheval and Horse Grenadiers in the rear, though greatly diminished in numbers. In a further push forward, the 18th came up against the troops of Cuirassiers and Lancers as well as infantry and guns, and were repulsed by a square on the top of a nearby knoll. However, the British cavalry soon regained the initiative and finally carried the day.

'I never saw such a day', wrote Sir Hussey Vivian. 'I expect . . . that every soldier will bear a medal with Mont St Jean on it'. ('Mont St Jean' was the first name proposed for the battle.)

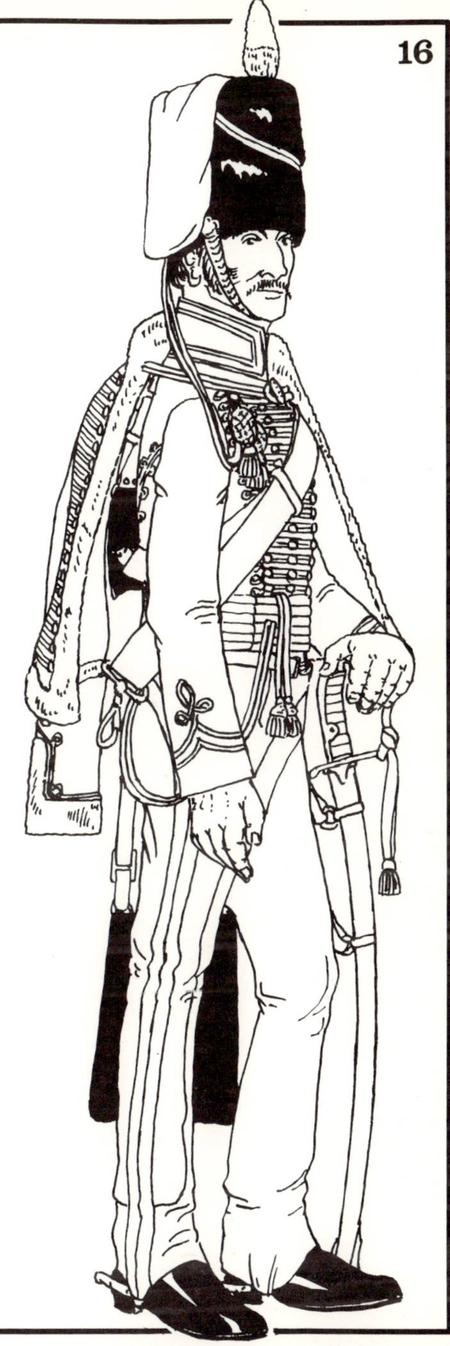

*(16) 7th Hussars. Trooper. Fur busby with red bag, white cords and a white over red plume. Jacket dark blue with white cords. Pelisse dark blue with white cords and edged all round with grey fur. Barrel sash crimson with yellow barrels. Overalls grey with white stripes. All belts white, sabretache black.*

(17) 15th Hussars. Trooper. Red shako with a wide white band round the top, plume white over red, yellow cords. Jacket dark blue with red collar and cuffs, all cords and piping white, dark blue pelisse edged with black fur, white cords. Barrel sash crimson with yellow barrels. Overalls grey with double red stripes. Shabraque was dark blue with a red vandyke edge, the devices on the front and rear ends were all red. (18) 18th Hussars. Trooper. Light brown fur busby with a light blue bag, white over red plume, white cords. Jacket dark blue with white collar and cuffs and white cords, pelisse dark blue with white cords, edged all round with white fur. Barrel sash blue and white. Overalls grey with white stripes. Shabraque dark blue with a white border.

(19 10th Hussars. Officer. Fur busby with red bag and gold cap lines, white over red plume. Jacket dark blue with red collar and cuffs, all lace and buttons silver. Pelisse dark blue with silver cords and buttons, pelisse edged all round with white fur. Grey overalls with a double red stripe down each side seam. The barrel sash was crimson with gilt barrels.

# Artillery



Originating from 1793, the Royal Horse Artillery was formed to provide mobile artillery support for the cavalry, and therefore all personnel was mounted.

The crested helmet of 1815 was slightly larger than the original model, but the laced jacket was of distinct hussar inspiration, a curious convention which affected the dress of the Horse Artillery in a number of countries.

It was to this branch that Congreve's Rocket Troop was attached – an entirely new development in the field of firearms. Rocket gunners carried a bundle of rocket-sticks in a small bucket forward of the offside stirrup and four 6-pounder rockets in two specially constructed holsters. An effective drill was devised, and the weapon, though perhaps not as deadly as expected, had considerable demoralizing value. It was, of course, the forerunner of the huge long-range rockets of today.

The Foot Artillery was much older than the Horse, having been founded on May 26, 1716, in replacement of the 'trains of artillery' which used to be raised at the start of a campaign and disbanded at its close. It became a Royal regiment in 1722 and has remained so to this day.

The uniform, except in its early years, was always blue, with red facings, so that by the time of Waterloo a gunner looked like an infantryman in reversed colours: 'belgic' cap, laced jacket and blue-grey trousers, or white breeches and black gaiters for home duty.

The artillery drivers belonged to a separate corps and wore a uniform combining the yellow-laced, square-cuffed jacket of the Foot Artillery with the helmet and overalls of the Horse branch.

The total number of Royal Artillery troops engaged at Waterloo amounted to 48 guns and 1,400 men in the Horse Artillery, and 54 guns and 3,630 men in the Foot.

*(20) Royal Horse Artillery. Helmet white plume, blue turban, brass fittings. Jacket, blue, scarlet collar and cuffs, yellow lacing and chevrons, brass buttons, crimson sash. Overalls grey, scarlet stripes. Belt, Gloves, Slings, white. Sword, all-steel, white knot (after Denis Dighton, in Reynolds MSS)*

(21) Royal Horse Artillery. Driver and Gunner. Helmets, white plume, blue turban, brass fittings. Jackets, blue, scarlet collar, cuffs, shoulder-straps, turnbacks, yellow lacing, brass buttons. Overalls, grey, scarlet stripes, white buttons. Sword, all-steel, white knot. (after Macdonald 'Hist. Dress R.A.'' and Reynolds MSS).

(22) Royal Regiment of Artillery. Field Officer, 1815. Shako, white plume, gilt plate, gold cords. Jacket, blue, scarlet collar, lapels, cuffs, turnbacks. Gold loops and buttons. Sash, crimson. Breeches, gloves, white. Sword, gilt fittings, gold knot.

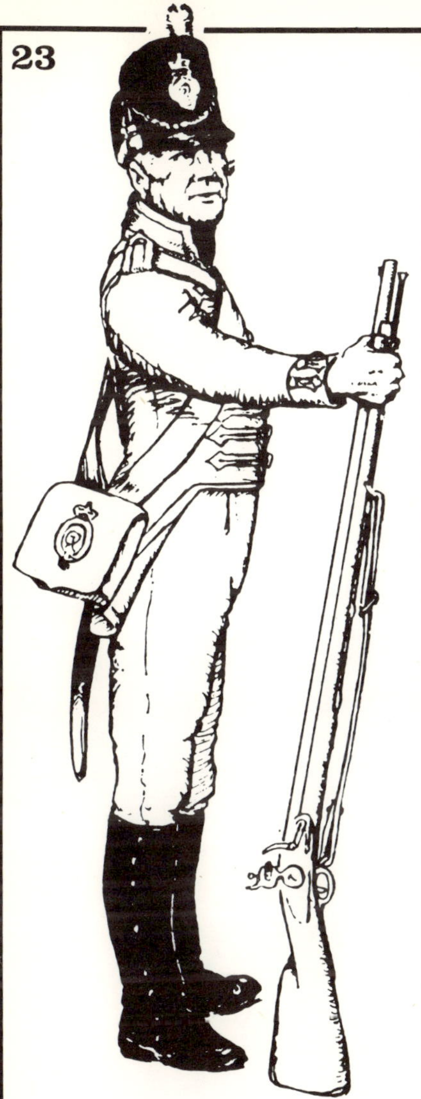

(23) *Royal Regiment of Artillery. Gunner, 1814. Shako, white ornaments, brass plate. Jacket, blue, scarlet collar, shoulder-straps, cuffs, turnbacks, yellow lace, brass buttons. Belts, breeches, pouch, white, brass plate. (after Hamilton Smith, 'Cost. of Army').*

# Foot Guards



The original Foot Guards of the Restoration were raised partly for ceremonial duties in London, partly for active service abroad; and it is interesting to observe that from the very start they were dressed in red coats.

These, then, were the 1st Foot Guards (now the Grenadier Guards). The 2nd Regiment was originally a unit of the Parliamentarian army; but in January 1660, from its station at Coldstream, it marched to London as Monk's Regiment of Foot to assist in the Restoration of Charles II on his return to England from the Netherlands. The regiment, henceforth based on the capital, not unnaturally became known to the inhabitants as 'the soldiers from Coldstream' and has never relinquished that title, though in a different form.

The 3rd Foot Guards were descended from a regiment reputedly raised as long ago as 1642. Its early history, however, is obscure; but it was not until 1877 that Queen Victoria restored its original title of The Scots Guards.

By 1815 the three regiments were brigaded together as The Guards Brigade and wore the regulation red infantry jacket of the British Army. The facings, on collar, cuffs and shoulder-straps, were of the dark blue reserved for Royal regiments, and the breeches were white, worn with black under-knee gaiters. On active service, however, these were exchanged for blue-grey trousers.

The shako, of regulation 'belgic' pattern, was often enclosed in an oilskin cover, but on dress occasions it was ornamented with white cords for the grenadier and battalion companies, and green for the light infantry. On ceremonial duties, the grenadiers wore a bearskin cap with a brass plate in front. Plumes were white for grenadiers, white-over-red in the battalions, and green for the light companies.

The flank companies (i.e. grenadiers and light infantry) were further distinguished by wings worn at the tip of the shoulders, whereas the battalion companies simply had a tuft of white worsted. It was on the jacket, too, that the regimental distinctions appeared, since the 1st

(24) *This officer of the 1st Foot Guards is wearing full dress: an all-scarlet coat with gold lace epaulettes, white breeches, gaiters, belt and gloves, and a crimson sash. The plume is white and the cap-plate gilt. This is the dress of the grenadier company.*

Foot Guards wore their buttons – and the attendant loops – equally spaced, while in the 2nd they were in pairs, and in threes in the 3rd. These loops were of 'bastion' shape (i.e. ending in a point shaped like a pike or an arrow-head) in the 1st Guards, but ending in a plain point in the other two regiments.

The Guards Brigade's main action at Waterloo was its stubborn defence of Hougoumont Farm on the right of the Allied line. The buildings, situated as they were in the low ground between the two armies, formed a major strongpoint whose possession became a vital asset on the terrain. The Guards held on grimly throughout the battle, in spite of repeated and heroic attempts by French infantry to break down the gate. Indeed, we shall see further that an officer of the 1st Light Infantry actually effected a breach, but was killed in the process.

*(25) Sergeant. 2nd Foot Guards. The jacket is scarlet, as for officers; and the plume white-over-red, denoting a battalion company. For grenadiers it would be white, and for the light company green. Note the pike (replacing the 18th century spontoon) which was the normal weapon for sergeants.*

*(26) Private. 1st Foot Guards. The equipment would normally include a blue water-bottle and white haversack on the left hip.*

The British infantry regiments, unlike the French, were each distinguished by special characteristics of dress. Every one had its particular facing colour and lace, as well as its own arrangement of buttonhole loops (either in singles or in pairs) which could be in three shapes: pointed, square-ended or bastion. In addition, officers' epaulettes and lace could be either gold or silver. Thus every regiment looked different from its neighbour; and where, in spite of this, duplication still existed, the colour of the lines in the lace would mark the difference. Bandsmen frequently wore reversed colours (Fig 15).

An interesting feature is the fact that the 91st, although Highlanders, did not wear the kilt. This was restored to them in 1821 and they eventually became the 1st Battalion of the Argyll and Sutherland Highlanders. They were one of the regiments detailed to watch over Napoleon at St Helena, and the Emperor was very complimentary to all ranks.

A detailed account of the various actions of the Line regiments is impossible in this short exposition; but their place in the order of battle will be found elsewhere in this book, and the serious student is referred to the numerous regimental histories which are readily available.

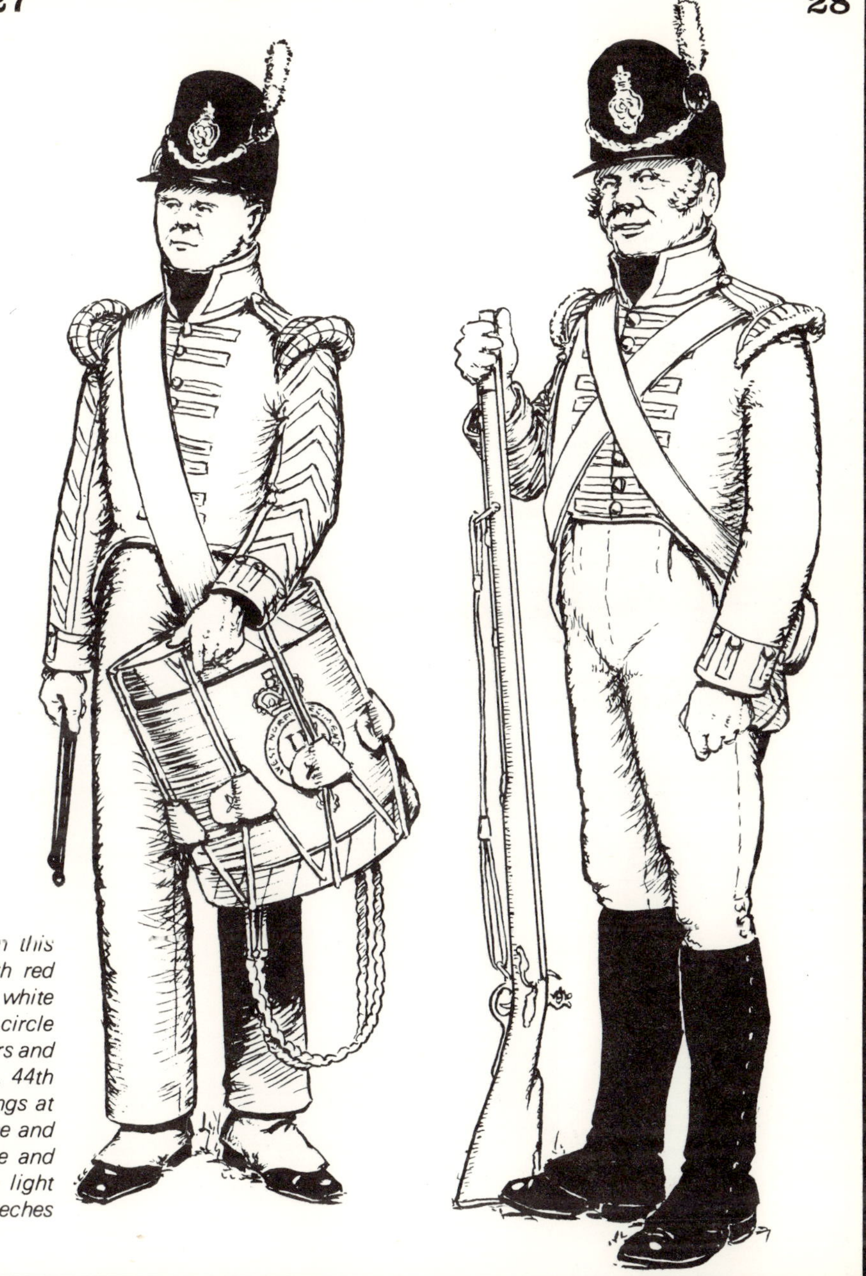

*(27) Drummers frequently wore reversed colours' in this case – the 54th Foot – a bright green jacket with red facings. The drum, too, is green, with red and white diagonals on the hoops. The central design is a blue circle enclosed in a red ring. All lace is white, and the trousers and gaiters are the regulation blue-grey. (28) Grenadier. 44th Foot. Flank companies were distinguished by red wings at the shoulders. These were trimmed in regimental lace and carried a short white fringe at the edge. The plume and cords were white for grenadiers and green for the light companies. This figure is wearing the white breeches prescribed for home duty.*

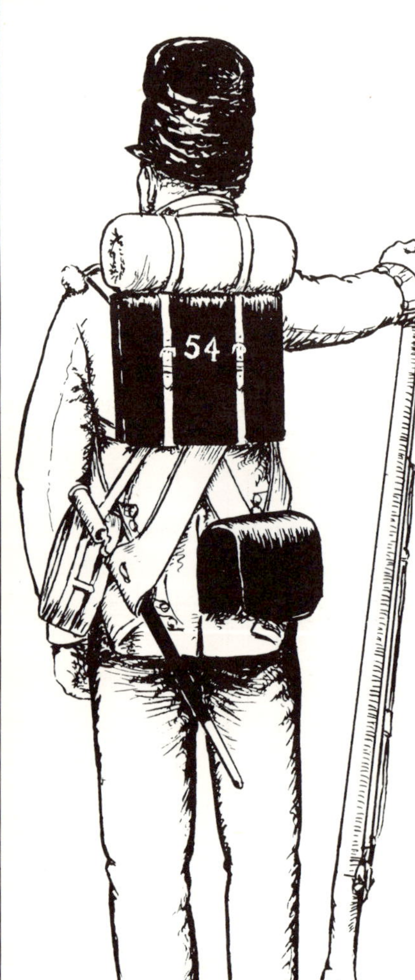

(29) Private. 54th Foot. Most units wore an oilskin cover over their shakos on the day of the battle because of the heavy thunderstorms that prevailed. Packs were not subject to regulations, and regiments generally made their own arrangements, in most cases painting the numeral on the outer flap.

Thus, the dress of the British Line regiments engaged at Waterloo can be summed up as follows:

| Regiment | Facings | Loops | Officers's Lace |
|---|---|---|---|
| 1st | blue | pairs, square | gold |
| 4th | blue | singles, bastion | silver |
| 14th | buff | pairs, square | silver |
| 23rd | blue | singles, bastion | gold |
| 25th | blue | singles, bastion | gold |
| 27th | buff | singles, square | gold |
| 28th | yellow | pairs, square | silver |
| 30th | light yellow | singles, bastion | silver |
| 32nd | white | pairs, square | gold |
| 37th | yellow | pairs, square | silver |
| 40th | buff | pairs, square | gold |
| 44th | yellow | singles, square | silver |
| 54th | green | pairs, square | silver |
| 59th | white | singles, bastion | gold |
| 69th | green | pairs, square | gold |
| 73rd | dark green | singles, bastion | gold |
| 78th | buff | singles, bastion | gold |
| 81st | buff | pairs, pointed | silver |
| 84th | yellow | pairs, square | silver |
| 91st | yellow | pairs, square | silver |

(30) Grenadier Officer. 28th Foot. Note the wings (silver in this regiment) of the Grenadier Company. The Grenadier Officer's sword is really slightly curved, though this is not readily apparent in this view.

(31) Officer. 1st Foot. This is the senior line regiment of the British Army: The Royal Scots. A single epaulette on the right shoulder denotes an officer of the battalion companies, and the dark blue facings a Royal regiment. (32) Private. 4th Foot. This soldier belongs to a battalion company, and his plume therefore, is white-over-red. The worsted shoulder-tufts are white.

# Highlanders

Three regiments of kilted Highlanders took part in the battle: the 42nd (The Black Watch), the 79th (The Queen's Own Cameron Highlanders) and the 92nd (2nd Battalion The Gordon Highlanders).

The 42nd and 92nd were brigaded together in the 9th Brigade, under Sir Denis Pack, with the 1st Foot (The Royal Scots) and the 2nd Battalion of the 44th. The 79th was the only Scottish regiment in Sir John Kempt's 8th Brigade. All these splendid regiments, which had seen heavy fighting at Quatre Bras, were now posted on the left centre of the Allied line, where they were drawn up, in greatly diminished numbers, just north of the Ohain road – that fateful sunken road where so much fighting occurred, to the east of La Haye Sainte.

The French infantry advanced as far as the hedge bordering this road and then halted to gather strength for their final charge, when the 92nd were ordered to attack with the bayonet. Picton then sent his whole division forward, and as he led the charge he was shot dead. It was at that moment that the Union Brigade came through to carry out their impetuous attack, and some of the Highlanders, in a somewhat undisciplined burst of enthusiasm, grasped the Greys' stirrup-leathers and charged with them.

The Black Watch (42nd), the oldest of the Highland regiments, was descended from the independent companies of Scottish gentlemen raised in the early 17th century to keep order in the Highlands. Their name, often explained as reflecting the dark colour of their tartan, really derives from the original duty of the Watch, namely to prevent marauding bands of Highlanders from collecting 'black meal' from the inhabitants. This was a highly illegal levy, demanded with menaces, and the word has now passed into current speech as 'blackmail'.

The 79th was raised by Cameron of Erracht in 1793, and was thus only 22 years old when it fought at Waterloo – the same age, incidentally, as the Royal Horse Artillery. After being in action at Quatre Bras on June 16, the regiment

bivouacked on the night of the 17th in the rain-sodden fields near La Haye Sainte. Next morning, the French began the attack at about 10.30, with their infantry bearing down on the 79th and 28th. They were successfully repulsed, but Napoleon now brought up his cavalry. The 79th formed square, and then, to their surprise and admiration, Piper Kenneth Mackay stepped out of the ranks to cheer his comrades with the strains of 'Cogadh na Sith'.

The 79th suffered heavily in the battle, for out of the 43 officers and 735 other ranks that set out from Brussels three days earlier, only 9 officers and 288 men remained to bivouack at La Belle Alliance that night.

*(33) Colour-Sergeant. 42nd Foot. The scarlet jacket has a blue collar, shoulder-straps and cuffs; and the kilt is of the sombre 'Government Tartan' peculiar to the Black Watch. The sash, knotted on the right, is crimson, and the hose are white with pink stripes, the colour-sergeant's rank-badge, on the right sleeve only, consists of a Union Flag and crossed swords in full colour beneath a crown and above a single white chevron. The bonnet has a red, white and black dice-border and a red hackle. (34) Officer. 79th Foot. The facings here – on collar, lapels and cuffs – are of a dark but bright green, and the lace, epaulettes and buttons are gold. The plume is white-over-red, and the hose as in the 42nd. The tartan of the 79th is a colourful sett predominantly dark blue, but with a generous proportion of red and a distinctive yellow line. Buttons were in distinct pairs, not apparent here where they are partly obscured by cross-belts. (35) Corporal. Grenadier Company, 92nd Foot. Whereas officers' and sergeants' jackets were scarlet, those of the other ranks were red. The wings and white hackle proclaim the grenadier, but for the rest the uniform is the regulation other ranks' pattern. The facings are yellow and the kilt much resembles that of the 42nd except that here a yellow line is present in the pattern, forming large squares.*

# Light Infantry

As a fairly recent development in the British Army, the light infantry was first organized by Sir John Moore during his service in Minorca (1803) on the pattern of the French *voltigeurs*, after he had observed Major Mackenzie's system of breaking up a battalion into skirmishers, supports and reserves. He therefore introduced the system in his own regiment, the 52nd.

The uniform of these troops was almost identical with that of the light companies of the Line battalions, except that the shako was replaced by a black felt 'conical' cap.

Three light infantry regiments were present at Waterloo: the 51st (later The King's Own Yorkshire Light Infantry), the 52nd (later the 2nd Battalion The Oxfordshire and Buckinghamshire Light Infantry) and the 71st (The Highland Light Infantry). Their jackets were of regulation infantry pattern, with blue facings for the 51st and buff for the other two. The loops were pointed and in pairs for the 51st, square in pairs for the 52nd, and square in singles for the 71st; and the officers wore gold lace in the 51st and silver in the others. However, the 71st wore dark blue caps in the rank and file, with the diced border peculiar to Scottish regiments.

The 51st was in the 4th Brigade, with the 14th and 23rd Foot, on the extreme right of the Allied line, west of the Nivelle road, and therefore was not heavily engaged. After the battle, however, they entered Hougoumont Farm, where Wheeler, the diarist, records, 'I had the honour of cooking a beefsteak in the steel jacket belonging to one of the Cuirassiers'.

The 52nd, also in position near Hougoumont, did not come into action until the close of the battle, when they were attacked by the 3rd Foot Chasseurs in that last and vital action of the Imperial Guard. However, with the 71st they formed square and eventually joined in the final advance after the commanding officer, Sir Colin Colbourne, had initiated the brilliant flanking movement which, according to some, ensured the victory.

*(36) 52nd Foot. The private is carrying the light infantry musket which was introduced about this time, but probably not used at Waterloo; while the officer wears silver wings and the curved light infantry sword.*

*(37) 71st Highland Light Infantry. Sergeants of light infantry wore their sashes cross-wise and carried a whistle on the cross-belt. Their chevrons appeared on both sleeves and instead of a pike, as in the line, they were armed with a short musket. The bugler wears reversed colours.*

# The Rifle Brigade

The only British rifle regiment at Waterloo was the 95th (The Rifle Brigade) whose sombre green and black uniform formed a marked contrast with the red coats of the Line.

This was the corps that was raised at the turn of the century and numbered 95th in August 1800. It was modelled on the 60th (The King's Royal Rifle Corps), a body descended from the 5th Battalion of The Royal American Regiment: a special battalion of light troops designed to counteract the activities of the American Rangers in the War of Independence. It was dressed in dark green, after the style of the German Jaegers, and its drill and tactics were devised on lines hitherto unheard of, for the soldier was taught to think for himself, to be self-reliant and to act on his own initiative, rather than to move in the dense formations of the Line.

The Rifles had been hardly pressed at Quatre Bras, and again at Waterloo, when two companies found themselves in the thick of the fighting in a gravel pit near La Haye Sainte. So fierce were the French attacks that the riflemen were unable to maintain contact with the defenders inside the buildings and were forced to withdraw. At about 3 o'clock, however, they regained possession of a mound near the farm, but were later driven off when the French captured the position. Yet they soon reformed and put up a stout defence against the repeated charges of the Cuirassiers.

*(continued on page 26)*

1. 1st Dragoon Guards, Trooper.   2. 1st Royal Dragoons, Trooper.   3. 6th Inniskilling Dragoons, Officer.   4. 7th Hussars, Trooper.   5. 10th Hussars, Trooper.   6. 15th Hussars, Trooper.

(38) *The green uniform of these troops was so dark that it appeared almost black; but the most curious feature is the unaccountable fashion for officers of this corps to copy the hussar dress. The Baker rifle shown here was much shorter than the 'Brown Bess' and the grooved bore of the barrel imparted a spin to the bullet, as in present-day weapons. The rifle would not accommodate a bayonet, so riflemen, then as now, 'fixed swords'.*

# Staff Corps, Engineers and Transport

The Cavalry Staff Corps was raised in April 1813 to act as a form of military police and to undertake the orderly duties previously performed by cavalrymen detached from their units.

The Corps was dressed in a light dragoon uniform, but here the jacket was scarlet with blue facings, and the overalls had a double blue stripe (Fig 11). The horse-furniture consisted of a small saddle-cloth with a narrow white border, surmounted by a circular red valise bearing the initials 'S.D.' on the ends, above the letter of the particular troop. A grey cloak was rolled and strapped over the pommel of the saddle.

The Staff Corps was disbanded in 1814, but hurriedly re-raised in the following year after Napoleon's sudden return from Elba.

There was also a dismounted branch of the Corps, but it is not clear whether it served in the present campaign. The uniform was of infantry pattern, with a grenadier's white plume on the shako, but the red jacket was a plain single-breasted garment without any loops. Cuffs, collar and shoulder-straps were dark blue, the last two items edged in white lace. A white cross-belt ran over the left shoulder and the dress was completed by a white waist-belt with a brass plate. The breeches were dark blue, encased in black mid-calf gaiters.

In the early days of military engineering, the appropriate organization consisted entirely of officers. They were later assisted by a separate body of military artificers which subsequently became the Royal Corps of Sappers and Miners (Fig 13). The officers, however, remained a different entity, entitled The Royal Engineers and originally dressed in blue. Early in the Napoleonic Wars, however, this often caused them to be mistaken for French officers and in consequence the uniform was changed to scarlet (Fig 12).

Another vital service, the transport, was represented at Waterloo by units of the Royal

Waggon Train. Few bodies of the British Army have so many times changed their title and dress: Corps of Waggoners; Royal Waggon Train; Land Transport; Commissariat Corps; Army Service Corps, and finally the present-day Royal Corps of Transport being among the titles.

The Royal Waggon Train dated from 1799, and was clothed in a blue uniform and raised for service in the North Holland Expedition under the command of a Waggon Master General with the rank of lieutenant-colonel. It was formed from men drafted from various cavalry regiments, the junior officers being mostly former troop quartermasters and sergeants. In 1811 the colour of the jacket was altered to red (Fig 14) and by 1814 there were 14 troops in existence, with a total of 1,903 other ranks; but despite its fine record of service the Corps was disbanded at Hythe in March 1833 after having served in the two Peninsular Wars as well as at Waterloo.

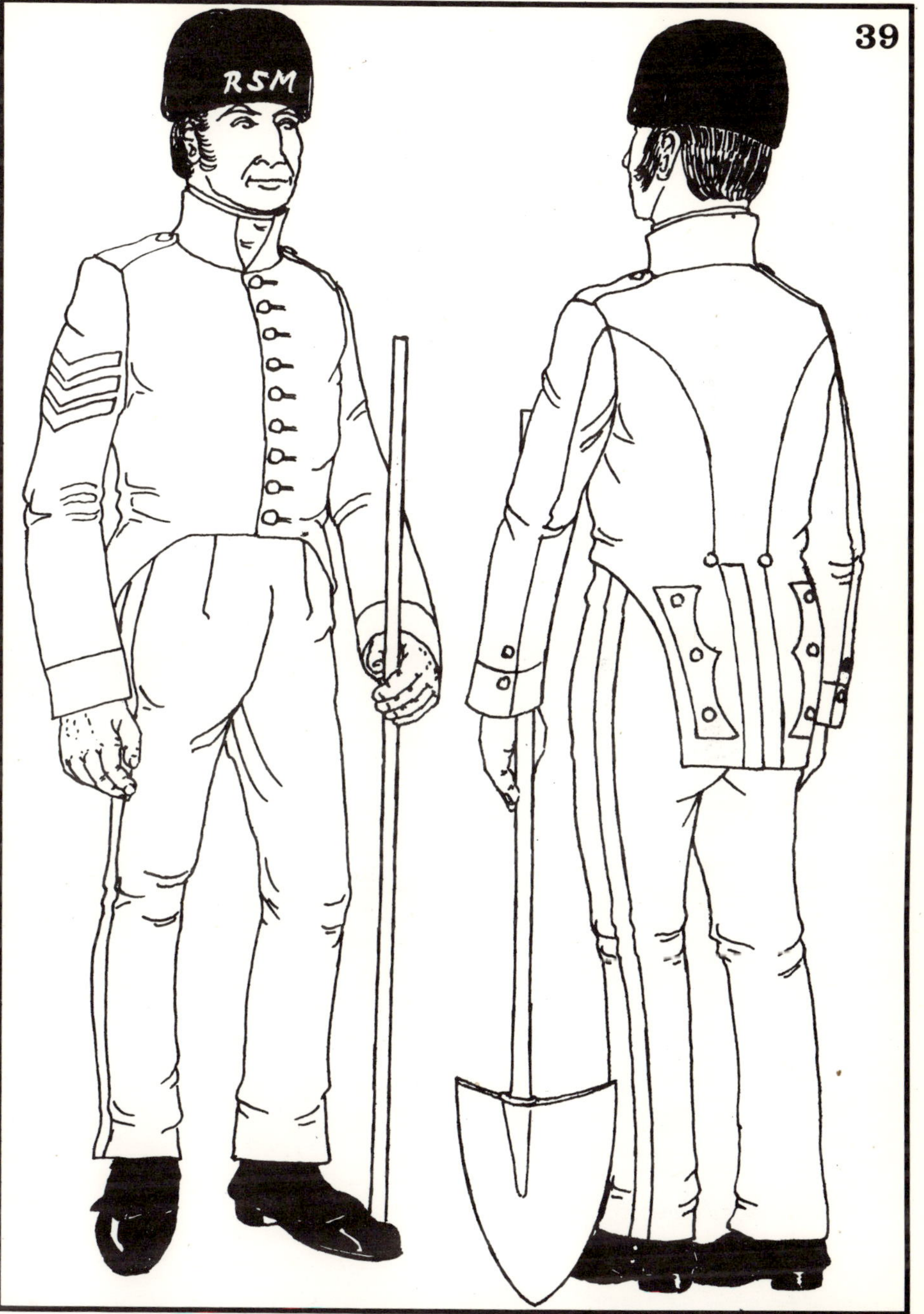


*(39) Royal Sappers and Miners. Sergeant and Sapper in working dress. Head-dress a black leather cap with front and rear flaps, the front lettered R.S.M. in yellow. Coat red with dark blue collar and cuffs and yellow metal buttons. Grey overalls with a wide red stripe.*

*(continued on page 30)*

7. 18th Hussars, Trooper. 8. 1st Hussars (KGL), Trooper. 9. 2nd Hussars (KGL), Officer. 10. 3rd Hussars (KGL), Trooper. 11. Royal Staff Corps, Private. 12. Royal Engineers, Officer.

13. Royal Sappers & Miners Sapper. 14. Royal Wagon Train, Private. 15. 30th Foot Drummer. 16. Bremen & Verden Hussars, Trooper. 17. Lüneberg Hussars, Trumpeter. 18. Cumberland Hussars, Trooper.

(40) *Royal Engineers – Officer. Head-dress black with gold loop and button, white feather plume. Coat scarlet with dark blue collar, cuffs, and lapels, white turnbacks, gold lace on collar, cuffs and lapels, gold epaulettes. Grey overalls with a gold stripe on outer seams. Sash crimson. Sword belt white.*

(41) *Royal Wagon Train – Officer. Black shako with band of silver lace round top, silver cords, white over red plume, Jacket scarlet with dark blue collar and cuffs, white turnbacks, lace and buttons silver. Sash crimson, white sword belt. Overalls grey with brown leather inserts, silver stripe down each side seam.*

(42) *Cavalry Staff Corps. Black head-dress with band of white lace round top edge, white cords and red plume. Jacket red of light dragoon pattern with dark blue collar, cuffs, turnbacks and plastron all edged with a narrow white lace. Girdle alternate stripes Blue, Red Blue, Red, Blue. Pouch belt and sword belt white, overalls dark grey with double blue stripes.*

# The King's German Legion; Light Dragoons



During the Continental wars of 1801-6, the Kingdom of Hanover, closely associated as it was with the British Crown, found itself in an extremely uneasy position, being occupied alternately by France and Prussia. Small wonder, then, that attempts were made to regain contact with Great Britain by encouraging a more or less clandestine enlistment of recruits for the British service.

Thus, on August 10, 1803, King George III charged Baron Decken with the raising of a corps of light infantry to be called The King's Germans. By November, 450 recruits had arrived in the Isle of Wight, and, as prospects seemed encouraging, it was resolved to extend the establishment to cavalry and artillery as well, and to name the entire force The King's German Legion.

The first cavalry units were equipped as heavy dragoons, but these were later converted to two regiments of light dragoons and dressed much as their British counterparts. The uniform was substantially the same in both regiments, the only difference being gold/yellow ornaments for the 1st, and silver/white ones for the 2nd.

At Waterloo, both these regiments, brigaded together with the British 23rd Light Dragoons in Sir W. Dörnberg's 3rd Brigade, took little part in the early stages of the battle, but the 1st Regiment, after having been in second line behind the 3rd Division until about 2 p.m., was ordered at about 4 o'clock to assist the 23rd in repulsing the Cuirassiers harassing the British squares.

The 2nd Light Dragoons, also on the same mission, eventually joined the other two regiments in the final advance after 6 o'clock.

(43) Officers. 1st Light Dragoons. The left-hand figure is in the white breeches worn in full dress, while the other wears the overalls for field service. Note the unconventional shape of the sabretaches. (continued on page 34).

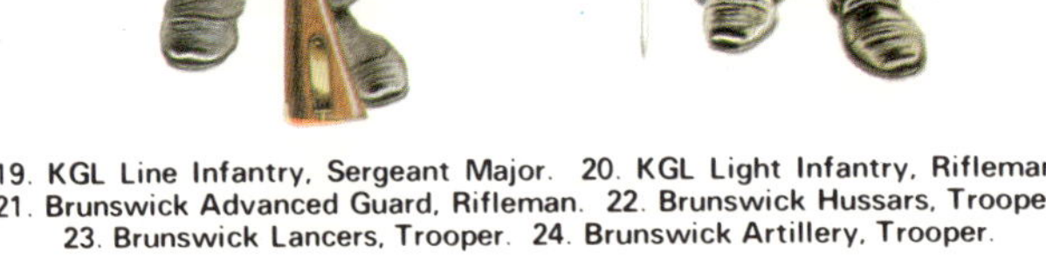

19. KGL Line Infantry, Sergeant Major.  20. KGL Light Infantry, Rifleman.
21. Brunswick Advanced Guard, Rifleman.  22. Brunswick Hussars, Trooper.
23. Brunswick Lancers, Trooper.  24. Brunswick Artillery, Trooper.

25. 1st Brunswick Infantry, Private.  26. Belgian Carabiniers, Trooper.
27. Dutch Belgian Artillery, Gunner.  28. Dutch Indian Infantry, Private.
29. Nassau Infantry, Private.

(44) Officer, 2nd Light Dragoons. The falling plume may be peculiar to this regiment. In full dress a dark blue sabretache was in use, with crowned Royal Cypher, scroll and border in silver embroidery, as shown in the detail close-up. (45 and 46) Privates, 1st and 2nd Light Dragoons. The style of dress is identical with the British light dragoons. Even the sword is the same and the only difference is in the colourings.

# The King's German Legion; Hussars and Artillery

The three hussar regiments of The King's German Legion were distinguished chiefly by their headdress: a black busby for the 1st (Fig 8), a brown one for the 2nd and a black shako for the 3rd (Fig 10). The pattern shown here (Fig 9) is a little unusual with its black leather peak, and appears to be peculiar to the K.G.L., since it was also worn by the rank-and-file in the 1st and in black fur by the officers of the 3rd.

The latter regiment, brigaded with the 3rd Light Dragoons in Colonel Arentschild's 7th Cavalry Brigade, was first stationed near La Haye Sainte in front of Ompteda's Brigade, but was forced to retire. South of Hougoumont, however, it later charged and broke a body of Cuirassiers, but was beaten back with heavy losses.

The 1st Hussars were with the 10th and 18th (British) Hussars in Sir Hussey Vivian's 6th Brigade, and the 2nd Hussars were with the 7th and 15th in Sir Colquhoun Grant's 5th Brigade.

The Horse and Foot Artillery uniforms were exact replicas of the British model, the only difference appearing in the Horse Artillery, where the red cuffs were cut square, and not pointed. These were edged along the top in yellow lace, which also described a wide round loop where one would normally expect a crow's foot or an Austrian knot. Another distinction was the white leather crossbelt, slung over the right shoulder, and bearing a brass buckle in the centre.

# The King's German Legion; Infantry of the Line

The infantry of the Legion, like the Light Dragoons and Hussars, was clothed in a uniform so closely resembling the British as to make identification almost impossible (Fig 19). But before examining the subject more closely, the following extract from N. Ludlow Beamish's *History of the King's German Legion* will prove interesting.

It is dated December 1803 and states: 'The original plan of forming one regiment only was now extended, and a corps consisting of cavalry, infantry and artillery was proposed to be raised. The better to effect this object, the independent levies of Colonel von der Decken and Major Halkett were ordered to be discontinued, and the men that had already been enlisted by those officers to be incorporated as the basis of a legion, which his majesty was pleased to authorize should be raised by his royal highness the Duke of Cambridge'.

# The King's German Legion; Light Infantry

There were two light infantry battalions in The King's German Legion, both dressed similarly to the British Rifle Brigade, except that in this case a pair of black wings was worn at the tip of the shoulders (Fig 20). The buttons were silver, and the only difference between the two units was the setting of these on the jacket, for in the 1st Battalion they appeared in one row of 12, in the 2nd there was one additional row on each side of the garment, running from the shoulders to the waist.

The officers of the 1st Battalion wore the same conical cap as the men, but their wings were the all-silver variety common to British light infantry officers. In the 2nd Battalion, however, the pattern was somewhat different. The headdress was a black 'Flügelmütze' or mirliton: that peculiar article much favoured by the early hussars and resembling, in this case, a regulation conical cap without a peak.

The jacket, in a very dark green, was ornamented with black hussar braiding, and the wings here were replaced by the same black cording retained by a silver button near the collar.

Officers wore white gloves, and their sash was of the wide crimson variety, worn around the waist and terminating in crimson cords and tassels after the manner of the British light infantry.

The K.G.L. light infantry battalions were in Colonel von Ompteda's 2nd Brigade (1st and 2nd Light Battalions, and 5th and 8th Line Battalions) in Sir Charles Alten's 3rd Division, while the remainder of the line battalions formed the 1st K.G.L. Brigade under Colonel du Plat (1st, 2nd, 3rd and 4th) in Sir H. Clinton's 2nd Division.

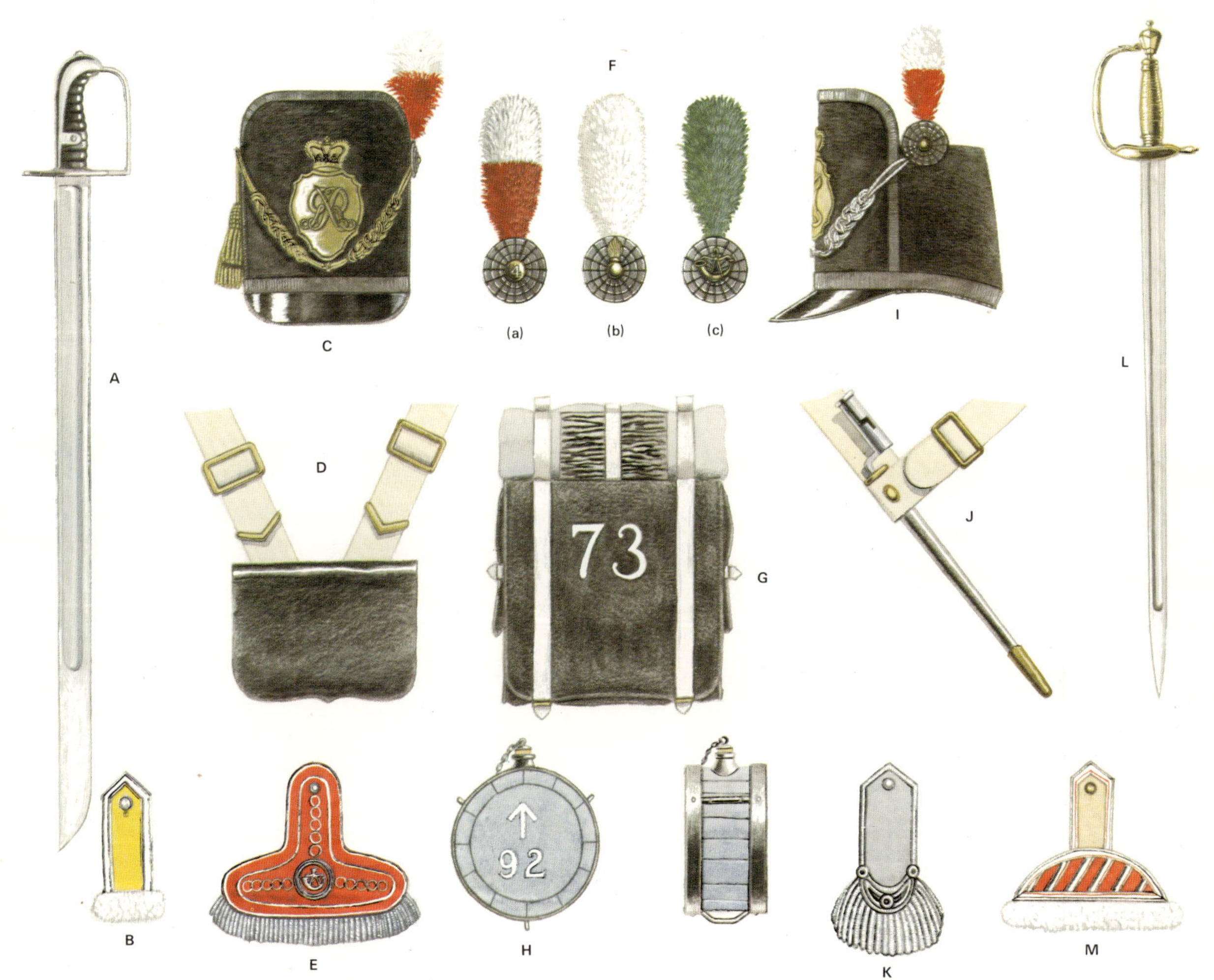

A. Heavy Cavalry Sword (OR's) 1796 pattern.  B. OR's shoulder Strap. Bn. Co. 44th Foot.  C. 'Belgic Cap' Officer (Bn. Co.).  D. Cartridge Box & Sling Attachment. E. Light Infantry Officer's Wing.  F. Cockades, (a) Bn. Co. 4th Foot, (b) Grenadier Co., (c) Light Co. G. Knapsack (painted canvas), Greatcoat & Mess Tin (73rd Foot).  H. Standard Issue Water Canteen.  I. 'Belgic Cap' Other Ranks.  J. Brown Bess Bayonet, Scabbard & Frog.  K. Captain. L. Infantry Officer's Sword, 1796 pattern. M. OR's wing Flank Co. 40th Foot.

# Hanoverian Hussars

until they reached Brussels, with the alarming news that the battle was lost. Schwertfeger, on the other hand, informs us with delightful *naïveté* that the commanding officer withdrew the regiment, 'but forgot to bring it back again'.

Three hussar regiments were raised in 1813: Lüneburg, Bremen-and-Verden and The Duke of Cumberland's Volunteer Hussars.

In the Bremen-and-Verden Regiment (Fig 16) the 1st and 4th Squadrons wore a bell-topped shako of British design, but the 2nd and 3rd had a brown fur busby with a tall white plume in front and cap-lines in the Guelphic colours of yellow and white. The busby-bag, hanging on the right, was red. For horse-furniture, this regiment had a green shabraque, to correspond with the green of the jacket, with a broad red border. There were no ornaments, and the round valise was green likewise, with a narrow red border at the ends.

The Lüneburg Hussars wore a blue jacket with a red collar and cuffs, and a red pelisse with white fur. The busby was similar to Bremen-and-Verden's except that the plume was red and the bag blue. Trumpeters wore reversed colours and white busbies with a red bag (Fig 17). The shabraque, ending in a sharp point as in the 1st Regiment, was blue and edged in red triangular vandykes, probably edged in white. Here again, no ornaments appeared on the shabraque.

The officers' uniform was basically the same as for the other ranks, except that the lacing was silver instead of white; but in what was known as 'gala' dress they wore red breeches with silver bands and Austrian knots, and a bicorne hat with a white plume.

The Cumberland Hussars (Fig 18), a unit of raw and inexperienced troops under an incompetent commanding officer, proved to be more of a liability than an asset. So long as they were held in reserve they were steady enough, but close action was not their *forte*. When the 3rd Hussars of the K.G.L. were driven back behind the squares after their charge near Hougoumont, Lord Uxbridge ordered the Cumberland Hussars to counter-attack; but their cautious approach to the enemy was so hesitant that the exalted Frenchmen, already elated by their previous success, not only stopped them, but sent them flying back in panic. According to Fortescue, they did not stop

**47**

**48**

*(47) Hannover. Bremen and Verden Hussars. Officer. Head-dress grey fur busby with green bag, white over red plume, gold busby lines. Dolman dark green with red collar and cuffs, collar and cuffs edged with silver lace, black cords, silver buttons. Pelisse red, black cords and silver buttons, edged with white fur (for other ranks pelisse red with white cords and black fur). Overalls dark green with black leather inserts, double red stripes on outer seams. Gold laced pouch belt, gold and white barrel sash, brown leather sword belt and slings, plain black sabretache, steel scabbard.*

*(48) Hannover. Luneberg Hussars. Trooper. Head-dress grey fur busby with light blue bag and white cords, white metal chin scales. Dolman dark blue with red collar and cuffs, white cords and white metal buttons. Pelisse red with white cords and fur. Barrel sash yellow and white. Overalls grey with red side stripes, black inserts. Pouch belt light buff. Sword belt and slings brown leather, scabbard steel, sabretache black.*

# Hanoverian Infantry and Artillery

Like their compatriots of The King's German Legion, the Hanoverian infantrymen were dressed in uniforms closely imitated from the British: red jackets and blue-grey trousers for the Line regiments and a very dark green for the rifle units, which were called light battalions. None of these appears to have been numbered, but they were known by such names as Bremen, Lüneburg, Grubenhagen, etc.

We find them mostly in the 1st Division under Lt-Gen. Sir Charles Alten, where six of these battalions formed Major-Gen. Count Kielmansegge's 1st Hanoverian Brigade, while in the 4th Division under Sir Colin Colville, five battalions made up Major-Gen. Sir Charles Lyon's 6th Hanoverian Brigade.

It was in the 4th Division, too, that the Hanoverian artillery served: Rettberg's and Braun's field batteries working alongside Brome's Royal Artillery troops and numbering a total of 12 guns. The gunners's uniform was probably based upon the British pattern, as in the K.G.L., although there is no concrete evidence to that effect.

To return to the infantry, it is interesting to note that several *Landwehr* units were employed. These were second-line troops – a kind of militia – and were to be found in the 3rd Hanoverian Brigade under Colonel Hew Halkett. Here, too, the units were known by name and not by number, and considerable variety in uniform appears from battalion to battalion. Most, however, seem to have worn the British type of dress, i.e., red for the line and dark green for the light; and the headdresses could be either a 'belgic' or light infantry cap. In other words, the same dress, practically, as the regular troops; and indeed, if any distinction did in fact exist, it was certainly not very evident.

*(49) Officer, Bremen Regiment. The position of the plume, in the front of the 'Belgic' cap, is odd, and may be a faulty recording by an eye-witness. The wings and cross-belt, also, seem out of place in a regiment not described as 'light'. (50) Officer, Luneburg Light Battalion. As in the K.G.L., the light infantry of the Hanoverian Army much resembled the British rifle regiments. However, The 'Belgic' cap shown here would not be worn by a British unit, nor would blue trousers. Note the Running Horse badge and the yellow sash peculiar to Hanover. (51) Sergeant, Grubenhagen Regiment. Another light infantry unit dressed after the British style. The sergeant's badge of rank appears to be the silver epaulettes.*

# Dutch-Belgian Cavalry

In 1815 the Dutch-Belgian cavalry, eight regiments strong, consisted of Carabiniers, Light Dragoons and Hussars, numbered consecutively, as in the British Army. Thus the 1st, 2nd and 3rd were Carabiniers, the 4th and 5th Light Dragoons, and the 6th and 8th Hussars. The 7th does not concern us here, because it was a colonial unit stationed in the East Indies. These units were formed mainly from individuals of the same nationality, so that the 1st and 3rd Carabiniers were Dutch and the 2nd Belgians, while in the light cavalry the 4th Light Dragoons and 6th Hussars were Dutch, and the 5th Light Dragoons and 8th Hussars Belgians.

The uniforms were of new design, because after Napoleon's first abdication in 1814, the Netherlands were restored to Austria, who appointed the Prince of Orange as Governor-General. In the southern provinces, a Belgian Legion had been formed on March 4 of that year and clothed in a uniform of Austrian pattern; but this was more in the nature of a stop-gap, since on August 20 regulations were promulgated for the raising of a truly national army under the auspices of the Sovereign Prince of the United States of the Netherlands.

Dress Regulations were approved on January 9, 1815, but by the month of June only a proportion of the troops had been issued with the new clothing. In fact, at Waterloo, many of them wore a transitional uniform, which probably accounts for many contradictions one encounters in even contemporary descriptions.

The Carabiniers wore a helmet of classical design, with a black fur crest and a brass plate in the form of a lion's head (Fig 26); but there is evidence that this was worn by the 2nd Regiment only, the Netherlanders still retaining their former bicorne hat.

The first two regiments were dressed alike, except that the 2nd wore red epaulettes, while the 1st had blue shoulder-straps piped red. In the 3rd the uniform was as in the 1st, but the collar was yellow.

In the Light Dragoons, the differences were more pronounced. The 4th wore a blue jacket with red collar, cuffs and turnbacks, and a black

*(52) Officer, 5th Light Dragoons. Here again the pattern of dress recalls in some measure the British model. The sash, however, is orange – the colour of the Dutch Reigning House.*

bell-topped shako with a tall black plume, while the 5th were in green with yellow facings and a green shako. The 4th had white breeches and the 5th grey.

Both Hussar regiments were dressed in light blue throughout (but the 6th had a red collar) and black shakos with a white plume. Buttons were of white metal in all regiments, and the lacing of the Hussars was correspondingly white. However, some sources show red shakos, and other a blue collar and red pointed cuffs.

During the battle, the Carabiniers were in the 1st Corps under the Prince of Orange, as part of the Dutch-Belgian Heavy Cavalry Brigade. At midday they were in reserve near Mont St Jean, between the Nivelles and Genappe roads, and up to about half-past three they were engaged in defensive manoeuvring. They soon passed to the attack, however, the 1st leading the charge, followed by the 2nd and 3rd.

The 4th Light Dragoons, at a strength of three squadrons, numbered about 700 all ranks under Lt-Col. Renno. It was part of the 2nd Light Cavalry Brigade, one of the three which made up General Baron Collaert's Cavalry Division.

The 5th, under Lt-Col. de Merx, was in the 3rd Brigade under van Merlen. The total strength was 441 men in two squadrons; but they were held in reserve at Waterloo, having suffered heavily at Quatre Bras, mostly at the hands of the French Chasseurs à Cheval, whose uniform, curiously enough was very similar to their own.

The two regiments of Hussars were also in Collaert's Cavalry Division: the 6th in the 2nd Brigade and the 8th in the 1st. The latter regiment, having been raised as late as November 1814, comprised mostly young and inexperienced soldiers. Many were of French and German nationalities, as well as Belgian, which further increased the difficulties of Colonel Louis Duvivier, the commanding officer.

It was soon in action against the Horse Grenadiers of the Guard – a singularly unfortunate situation for such raw troops. To make matters worse, an order to left wheel, given in Dutch, was misunderstood, and the regiment turned about to the joy of the French who pursued them hotly, inflicting heavy losses. Finally, reduced to the strength of a single squadron, it took part in Sir Hussey Vivian's and Vandeleur's cavalry movements in the closing stages of the battle.

*(53) Trumpeter. 8th Hussars. This is a soldier wearing reversed colours, the normal dress for the regiment being a light blue jacket with red facings.*

# Dutch-Belgian Artillery

In the Dutch-Belgian army the artillery consisted of nine batteries in all: 6 Dutch and 3 Belgian. Of these, the Belgians had one battery of horse artillery and two of foot (of which one – du Bois' – was in reserve), while the Dutch mustered two horse and four foot. All these units were equipped with 6-pounders except du Bois' which was a 12-pounder unit.

These troops wore the distinctive Netherlandish bell-topped shako, with a peak back and front, in close imitation of the Austrian headdress of the same period. The tall plume was black and the device in front took the form of crossed pieces in brass, surmounted by a crown in the same metal (Fig 28).

In the horse artillery the jacket was dark blue with a black collar and square cuffs of the same, bearing three-button slashes in the jacket colour. Shoulder-straps were blue, piped red, terminating in the characteristic Netherlandish padded wings of blue, with several lines of yellow piping. The garment was single-breasted and fastened by brass buttons; and the turnbacks were red, ornamented with blue grenades. The pockets at the back were simulated by a three-pointed line of piping with brass buttons in every angle. Grey overalls completed the outfit, with a red band bearing a row of brass buttons on the whole of its length.

The officers wore much the same, except that their collar and cuffs were made of velvet and the grenades on their turnbacks were gold, as were their epaulettes and overall-bands. The sash was orange, worn around the waist and knotted on the left hip.

Trumpeters appear to have worn either shakos or busbies. The former carried a white upright plume and the latter a red ball-tuft and bag, piped in yellow, with a tassel of the same colour. For the rest, the uniform was as above except for the epaulettes with a blue strap, edged and fringed in yellow. The trumpet cords, too, were yellow.

In the foot branch the dress was the same but for the absence of wings; and the drivers were distinguished by a red collar, shoulder-straps and cuffs, and white metal buttons. Some authorities, however, give a grey jacket instead of blue.

The Indian Brigade Artillery's uniform was somewhat different. The shako had no back peak and carried a red upright plume tipped black. The blue jeacket was like the British garment in cut, with its square cuffs and lapels. Collar, shoulder-straps, cuffs and turnbacks were scarlet; and the square-ended loops appearing on the collar, lapels and cuffs were yellow, to correspond with the brass buttons. Trousers and gaiters are shown as white, but these may well have been a tropical issue, replaced by grey for home service.

*(54) Dutch-Belgium Foot Artillery. Gunner. Head-dress black shako with orange cockade and yellow metal plate, red over black plume. Jacket dark blue, black collar and cuffs, cuff slash dark blue all with red piping, red turnbacks, yellow metal buttons. Trousers grey, gaiters black. Belts white, pack brown, grey rolled overcoat on top of pack, brass hilt to sword.*

*(55) Dutch-Belgium Horse Artillery. Gunner. Head-dress black shako with front and back peaks as foot gunner, orange cockade, yellow metal badge, red cords, black plume. Jacket dark blue with black collar and cuffs, three pointed cuff slashes dark blue, all piped red, red turnbacks, brass buttons, the shoulder roll wings red with narrow yellow lines. Belts white with yellow metal chain and prickets and waist belt plate. Overalls grey with black leather inserts, red stripe on outer seams. Sword with brass hilt and white sword knot, steel scabbard.*

# Dutch-Belgian Infantry

The infantry consisted of Dutch and Belgian units known respectively as North- and South-Netherlandish troops, differing in appearance mainly in the pattern of headdress, which for the latter was a 'belgic' shako (much resembling the British model), and a bell-topped variety, with peak back and front, for the former.

All battalions were dressed in single-breasted dark blue jackets and grey trousers, with collar, cuffs and piping in the facing colour, and nine brass buttons down the front. The turnbacks were red, while the cuff slashes were blue and the gaiters grey. The brass shako-plate, almost in the same design as the British, was stamped with the initial W in relief, and the plume and cords were white for the battalion companies and red for the flankers. The cockade for all troops was orange.

Flankers were further distinguished by large padded wings at the shoulders in the same cloth as the jacket, but bearing a number of white lines. The shoulder-straps – blue, with piping in the facing colour – were common to all companies.

Officers wore the same, but in finer cloth and with long skirts. Their shako-cords were of gold thread and they wore gold epaulettes, while their grey breeches were tucked into black Hessian boots. Gloves were white.

Drummers and fifers were dressed as the other ranks, but wore swallow-nests of a pattern peculiar to the Netherlands: a blue ground with two superimposed chevrons of white lace – one upright and the other inverted forming a diamond shape in the centre. There was a horizontal white lace at the base of the swallow-nest, and in some cases a white fringe below this. In some Belgian units, however, the swallow-nests were white with a yellow lace and fringe.

The Dutch-Belgian battalions were distinguished by the following facing colours, worn on the collar, cuffs and piping:

1st and 9th, orange; 2nd and 10th, yellow; 3rd and 11th, white; 4th and 12th, red; 5th and 13th, crimson; 6th and 14th, light green; 7th and 15th, light blue, and 16th, pink.

The light infantry were termed Chasseurs or Jagers and wore green jackets similar in pattern to the Line, but with light yellow facings. The same bell-topped shako was in wear, but here it carried a green plume and a brass bugle-horn plate with the battalion numeral in the circle. The 16th, 18th and 27th were Dutch, while the 35th and 36th were Belgian.

Several units of Militia were also present at Waterloo, dressed much as the Regulars except that their white metal shako-plate was in the form of a semi-circle of rays spreading from a horizontal base, with the battalion numeral in the centre. The 5th Battalion appears to have worn a conical cap with this plate, and a white plume. The buttons were of white metal for all the Militia.

The 'Indian' infantry wore the bell-topped shako with a light blue-over-white plume (Fig 27). The blue jacket had a light blue collar and lapels, with brass buttons and yellow loops, including two on each side of the collar and three on each cuff, which were of British pattern. Piping on the shoulder-straps, lapels, cuffs and turnbacks was red, as well as on the three-point pockets, which carried a yellow loop at each button. Trousers and gaiters were white, but it is possible that they were exchanged for grey when on service in Europe.

# Brunswick Cavalry and Artillery

The Brunswick Corps was part of the general reserve of the Netherlandish Army and consisted of one regiment of Hussars, one of Uhlans, two batteries of artillery and a body of infantry comprising three line battalions, three light battalions and one battalion of 'Avant-Garde' riflemen (Fig 21).

The whole of the Brunswick Army except the 'Avant-Garde' was dressed in the characteristic, essentially black uniform typical of that country. In fact, the British troops called them the 'Black Brunswickers'.

The Hussars, in black throughout except for light blue collars and cuffs, wore a white metal skull-and-crossbone device as a shako-plate (Fig 22). The origin of this badge is obscure: it has been used by the British 17th Lancers from very early days, and several German Hussar regiments wore it until 1918, while it also appeared in the Russian Army. In Great Britain it has been described as a memorial to the death of General Wolfe at Quebec, but a far more ancient origin seems likely. In the Brunswick Hussars the device was repeated on the black leather sabretaches of the rank-and-file, but for the officers it was replaced by the crowned cypher FW in gilt metal.

The Uhlans, in black likewise, wore the same light blue collar and cuffs as the Hussars (Fig 23). All this cavalry (i.e., the 2nd Hussars, of four squadrons under Major Cramm, and the 2nd Squadron of the Uhlans) formed a brigade of some 900 men.

The Artillery, also in the traditional black uniform, wore yellow facings in both the horse and foot branches (Fig 24). In the Horse Artillery the shako carried the black plume of the cavalry, as well as the skull-and-crossbones plate in white metal, but in the Foot these devices were discarded in favour of a yellow pear-shaped pompon and a white metal grenade.

(56) Fifer. In the infantry, musicians do not appear to have worn reversed colours, their only distinction being the characteristic Netherlandish swallows'-nests. (57) Private, 36th Chasseurs. Green was a favourite colour for light troops, and the bugle-horn badge to was the accepted emblem in many armies.

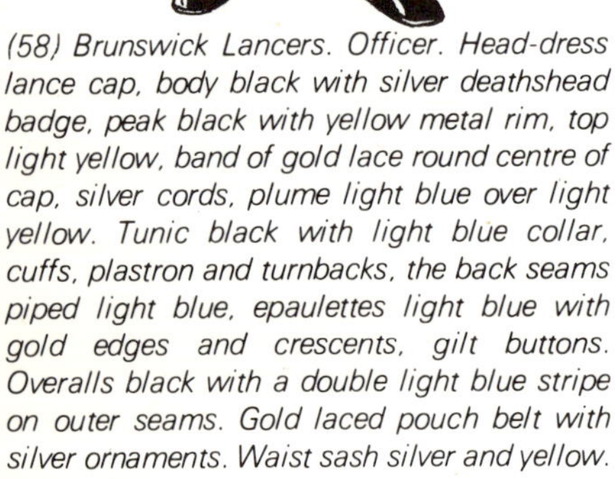

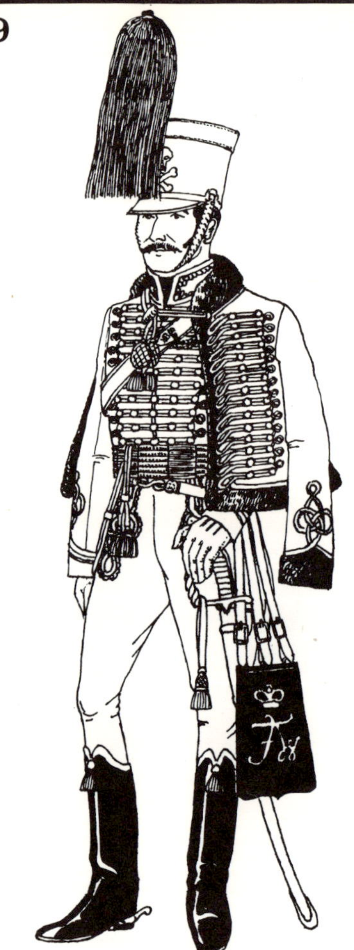

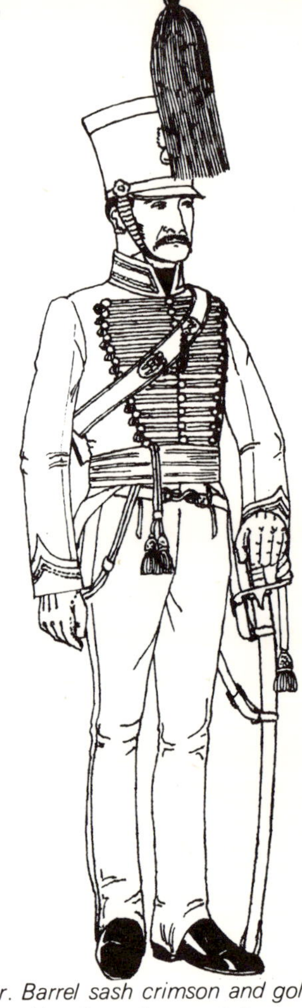

(58) Brunswick Lancers. Officer. Head-dress lance cap, body black with silver deathshead badge, peak black with yellow metal rim, top light yellow, band of gold lace round centre of cap, silver cords, plume light blue over light yellow. Tunic black with light blue collar, cuffs, plastron and turnbacks, the back seams piped light blue, epaulettes light blue with gold edges and crescents, gilt buttons. Overalls black with a double light blue stripe on outer seams. Gold laced pouch belt with silver ornaments. Waist sash silver and yellow.

Sword and scabbard steel, sword knot silver and yellow.

(59) Brunswick Hussars. Officer. Head-dress black with band of gold lace round top, gilt chin scales, silver deathshead badge and black hair plume. Dolman black with light blue collar and cuffs, all braid and buttons black. Pelisse all black edged in black fur. Breeches all black, boots black with gold lace round top, gold tassels, steel spurs. Pouch belt black edged gold with gilt plate. Sword belt and slings black, sabretache black with gilt

cypher. Barrel sash crimson and gold. Sword and scabbard steel, sword knot gold and crimson.

(60) Brunswick Foot Artillery. Officer. Head-dress black, badge, front edge of peak and chin scales gilt, black hair plume. Jacket black with gold lace on collar and cuffs, the lace traced inside with a line of gold tracing cord, black buttons. Overalls black with yellow stripes. Pouch belts and sword slings covered with gold lace. Waist sash silver and yellow, gloves white. Sword and scabbard steel, knot silver and yellow.

# Brunswick and Nassau Infantry

The three battalions of Brunswick Infantry of the Line were distinguished respectively by red facings for the 1st (Fig 25), green for the 2nd and white for the 3rd. The shako-plates, of white metal, were semi-circular in shape and stamped with the device of the White Horse of Brunswick and the motto *Nunquam Retrorsum*. This was surmounted by a small circle of the same metal bearing the battalion numeral, and the whole badge was worn high on the shako, partly covering the cockade.

The light infantry wore the same uniform but the shako here carried a white metal bugle-horn and a yellow-over-light blue pear-shaped pompon. The facing colours were: 1st Battalion, light blue (later pink-over-light orange), 2nd Battalion, yellow; and 3rd Battalion, orange.

Drummers of the Line units wore the same uniform as the other ranks plus swallows-nests at the shoulders. These were in the battalion facing colours (e.g., red for the 1st Battalion) and did not carry a fringe at the lower edge.

The Brunswickers were first stationed in the rear of the centre of the Allied line, but were subsequently called to the extreme right, and by evening were in action opposite Hougoumont when the Duke gave the order for the general advance.

The army of the Duchy of Nassau consisted at Waterloo of eight battalions of infantry: a contingent of some 7,000 men in all (Fig 30). Five of these battalions were incorporated in the Netherlandish Army, and the remaining three formed an independent brigade under the orders of General Kruse. The five battalions in Dutch service were grouped into two regiments: the Regiment of Orange-Nassau (28th of the Line in the Netherlandish Army) and the 1st Nassau Regiment.

The Regiment of Orange-Nassau and the 2nd Nassau Regiment were in Prince Bernard of Saxe-Weimar's 2nd Brigade of the 2nd Netherlandish Division under Lt-Gen. Perponcher: a part of the 1st Army Corps under the Prince of Orange.



(61) Brunswick Infantry. Officer 3rd Battalion. Head-dress black with black cockade and white metal badge, chin chain gilt metal, light blue over yellow plume. Jacket black with white collar, braid and buttons black. Trousers black with a white stripe. Waist sash silver and yellow. Sword belt and slings black, sword and scabbard steel, silver and yellow sword knot.

(62) Nassau Infantry. Grenadier 1st Regiment. Head-dress black fur busby. Jacket dark green with black collar, cuffs and shoulder straps all edged with yellow piping, red rolls on shoulders. Trousers dark green with a yellow stripe on outer seams, yellow darts on front flap. Black boots and gaiters. Belts light buff, sword and bayonet scabbards black with brass tips, bayonet with brass hilt and red strap and knot. Pack brown, overcoat roll grey. Musket slings light buff.

# APPENDIX 1: ORDER OF BATTLE; ANGLO-ALLIED ARMY, JUNE 18th, 1815

**Commander-in-Chief (Field-Marshal The Duke of Wellington)**

### I. Corps (The Prince of Orange)

*1st Division (Maj-Gen. Cooke)*
1st Brigade (Maj-Gen. Maitland) 1st Foot Guards.
2nd Brigade (Maj-Gen. Sir John Byng) 2nd Foot Guards, 2nd Bn. 3rd Foot Guards.
British and K.G.L. field batteries.

*3rd Division (Lt-Gen. Sir Charles Alten)*
5th Brigade (Maj-Gen. Sir Colin Halkett) 2/30th Foot, 33rd Foot, 2/69th Foot, 2/73rd Foot.
2nd K.G.L. Brigade (Col. von Ompteda) 1st and 2nd Light Bns., 5th and 8th Line Bns.
1st Hanoverian Brigade (Maj-Gen. Count Kielmansegge) 6 Hanoverian battalions.
British and K.G.L field batteries.

*2nd Netherlandish Division (Lt-Gen. Baron de Perponcher)*
1st Brigade (Maj-Gen. de Bijlandt) 5 Netherlandish Battalions.
2nd Brigade (Prince Bernard of Saxe-Weimar) 5 Nassau battalions.
1 Netherlandish horse battery.

*3rd Netherlandish Division (Lt-Gen. Baron de Chassé)*
1st Brigade (Maj-Gen. Detmers) 6 Netherlandish battalions.
2nd Brigade (Maj-Gen d'Aubremé) 6 Netherlandish battalions.

### II. Corps (Lt-Gen. Lord Hill)

*2nd Division (Lt-Gen. Sir H. Clinton)*
3rd Brigade (Maj-Gen. Adam) 1/52nd Foot, 1/71st Foot, 2/95th Foot, 3rd/95th Foot.
1st K.G.L. Brigade (Col. du Plat) 1st, 2nd, 3rd, 4th, Line battalions
3rd Hanoverian Brigade (Col. Hew Halkett) 4 Landwehr battalions.
British and K.G.L. field batteries.

*4th Division (Lt-Gen. Sir Colin Colville)*
4th Brigade (Col. Mitchell) 3/14th Foot, 1/23rd Foot, 51st Foot.
6th Hanoverian Brigade (Maj-Gen. Sir James Lyon) 5 Hanoverian battalions.
British and Hanoverian field batteries.

### Corps of Prince Frederick of the Netherlands

*1st Netherlandish Division (Lt-Gen. Stedman)*
d'Hauw's Brigade: 6 battalions
de Eeren's Brigade: 5 battalions.
1 field battery of 8 guns.
Anthing's Netherlandish Indian Brigade: 5 battalions.
1 field battery.

### Cavalry

1st Brigade (Maj-Gen. Lord E. Somerset) 1st and 2nd Life Guards, The Royal Horse Guards, 1st The King's Dragoon Guards.
2nd Brigade (Maj-Gen. Sir W. Ponsonby) Royal Dragoons, Scots Greys, Inniskilling Dragoons.
3rd Brigade (Maj-Gen. Sir W. Dörnberg) 1st and 2nd Light Dragoons of the K.G.L., 23rd Light Dragoons.
4th Brigade (Maj-Gen. Sir J. Vandeleur) 11th, 12th, 16th Light Dragoons.
5th Brigade (Maj-Gen. Sir Colquhoun Grant) 7th and 15th Hussars, 2nd Hussars of the K.G.L.
6th Brigade (Maj-Gen. Sir Hussey Vivian) 10th and 18th Hussars, 1st Hussars of the K.G.L.

7th Brigade (Col. Arentschild) 13th Light Dragoons, 3rd Hussars of
the K.G.L.
1 howitzer battery, 5 horse batteries.

| | |
|---|---|
| 1st Hanoverian Brigade | 3 regiments. |
| Brunswick Cavalry | 1 regiment + 1 squadron. |
| Netherlandish Cavalry | 3 brigades (Trip, de Ghingy, van Merlen) (i.e., 7 regiments + 2 half-batteries). |

### Garrisons

*7th Division*
7th Brigade, 2/25th Foot, 2/37th Foot, 2/78th Foot.
Hanoverian Reserve Corps, 12 Landwehr battalions in 4 brigade

### Reserve

*5th Division (Lt-Gen. Sir Thomas Picton)*
8th Brigade (Maj-Gen. Sir James Kempt) 1/28th Foot, 1/32nd Foot, 1/79th Foot, 1/95th Foot.
9th Brigade (Maj-Gen. Sir Denis Pack) 3/1st Foot, 1/42nd Foot, 2/44th Foot, 1/92nd Foot.
5th Hanoverian Brigade (Col. von Vincke) 4 Landwehr battalions
British and Hanoverian field batteries.
*6th Division*
10th Brigade (Maj-Gen. Sir John Lambert) 1/4th Foot, 1/27th Foot, 1/40th Foot, 2/81st Foot.
4th Hanoverian Brigade (Col. Best) 4 Landwehr Battalions.
2 British field batteries.
British Reserve Artillery: 2 horse batteries.
                                  3 field batteries.
*Brunswick Corps (The Duke of Brunswick)*
2 infantry brigades of 3 battalions each.
Advance Guard; 4 companies of infantry; 1 detachment of cavalry.
2 batteries of artillery.
*Nassau Contingent (Gen. von Kruse)*
3 battalions.

# APPENDIX 2: GLOSSARY OF TERMS

**Aiguillettes:** Ornamental cords, usually gold looped over one shoulder.

**Austrian Knot:** Sometimes called 'Hungarian knot'. An ornamental pattern of cording, usually worn on the cuff, arranged in large rings flanking a taller pointed shape in the centre.

**Belgic cap:** The British infantry shako introduced in 1811.

**Battalion companies:** The main body of an infantry battalion (see 'flank companies').

**Bell-topped shako:** A shako of inverted conical shape; i.e., wider at the top than at the bottom.

**Bicorne:** A two-cornered hat.

**Busby:** A fur head-dress worn by hussars and sometimes by horse artillery.

**Busby-bag:** A piece of coloured cloth, fitted to the top of a busby, and hanging to the side.

**Cap-lines:** The cords which connected the head-dress with the body. Sometimes called 'body-lines'.

**Cockade:** a rosette on the head-dress, often in national colours. In the British army it was black, and in the French, (from the centre) blue, red and white.

**Comb:** The curved plate of the upright metal surrounding a helmet.

**Conical shako:** The reverse of the bell-topped pattern; i.e., smaller at the top than at the bottom

**Crest:** A fur ornament, usually surmounting the comb.

**Dog's teeth:** The zig-zag edging of the cloth-lining under a sheepskin saddle.

**Elite Corps.** Picked troops.

**Facings:** The parts of the uniform, such as collar, cuffs etc, which are different in colour from the main garment.

**Flank companies:** The grenadier and light companies of an infantry battalion.

**Hessian boots:** Usually worn with hussar dress. The tops are cut in a heart-shaped pattern and often ornamented with lace and tassels.

**Jacket:** A short-tailed or tail-less garment, as opposed to a long tailed coat.

**Lace:** Strips of ornamental braiding, mostly used as an edging to collar, cuffs, etc, and also for buttonhole loops.

**Loops:** See above.

**Overalls:** Long trousers with an under-boot strap or chain, worn by mounted troops.

**Pack:** A soldier's knapsack, carried on the back.

**Pelisse:** The hussar's fur-trimmed jacket, slung over the left shoulder when not in wear.

**Piece:** A gun barrel.

**Piping:** The very narrow strips of coloured cloth, usually forming an edging to details of clothing, or marking the seams.

**Pompon:** A ball-tuft on the head-dress.

**Sabretache:** A pouch carried by cavalrymen, suspended by slings from the sword-belt.

**Shabraque:** A saddle-cloth with long rear points, often very ornate, usually used by light cavalry.

**Shako:** A rigid peaked head-dress.

**Shoulder-straps:** Cloth shoulder-pieces originally intended to keep the shoulder belts in position.

**Streamer:** The horsehair mane at the back of a heavy cavalry helmet.

**Swallows'-nests:** Cloth shoulder-ornaments, usually laced, denoting bandsmen.

**Turban:** The cloth or fur surrounding the base of a helmet.

**Turnbacks:** The parts of a coat-tail buttoned back to reveal the lining.

**Valise:** A case carried at the back of the saddle, containing the cavalryman's belongings.

**Wings:** Shoulder-ornaments in the form of a large crescent, usually denoting flank companies (in the British Army).